Junior NKIERE MAKOLONI

INFORMATION AND COMMUNICATION TECHNOLOGY (ICT) COURSE 8th EB

Junior NKIERE MAKOLONI

INFORMATION AND COMMUNICATION TECHNOLOGY (ICT) COURSE 8th EB

ScienciaScripts

Imprint

Cover image: www.ingimage.com

This book is a translation from the original published under ISBN 978-620-6-72560-2.

Publisher:
Sciencia Scripts
is a trademark of
Dodo Books Indian Ocean Ltd. and OmniScriptum S.R.L publishing group

120 High Road, East Finchley, London, N2 9ED, United Kingdom
Str. Armeneasca 28/1, office 1, Chisinau MD-2012, Republic of Moldova, Europe
Managing Directors: Ieva Konstantinova, Victoria Ursu
info@omniscriptum.com

Printed at: see last page
ISBN: 978-620-8-89630-0

PREFACE

Today's world is evolving at the pace of information technology and the Internet (information highways). All aspects of our society are governed by organization and administration, which are based on information technology. Information technology, which has been considered and used until now as a tool and support for certain subjects in national education, must become a subject of study in its own right. And this teaching can only be effective if it is based on materials that have been well written by an IT specialist and comply with the country's national curriculum.

This course will encourage students to adopt responsible behavior and demonstrate practical IT skills.

We would like to thank the Provincial Ministry of EPST Haut-Uélé and the Provincial Inspectorate of Haut-Uélé 2 for their involvement in the production of this book, which will be useful not only to the province of Haut-Uélé but also to all schools in our country that offer the Secretarial-Administrative option.

We recommend that schools fully appreciate the usefulness of IT and that they succeed in unlocking the mysteries of this new subject, which will enable Congolese children to become responsible individuals who are useful to themselves and to society.

SUMMARY

Many candidates in the orientation or retraining phase are attracted to the IT sector because of the wealth and diversity of opportunities it offers. This constantly evolving sector leaves room for innovation and offers many career opportunities. However, students need to be aware of the various disadvantages associated with this sector.

As we said in the previous book for the first year of humanities, Secretariat-Administration, the aim of secondary education is to provide students with general and specific knowledge to enable them to understand the elements of national and international cultural heritage. It also aims to develop their critical thinking, creativity, and intellectual curiosity, and to prepare them to choose their humanities subjects.

GENERAL OBJECTIVE

The general objective of this book is to provide 8th grade students with theoretical and practical knowledge of the basic concepts of computer science.

SPECIFIC OBJECTIVES

By the end of the course, all students who have attended regularly will be able to

to:

- Use the Word table;
- Insert geometric shapes using Word;
- Master mathematical symbols and equations in Word;
- Master arithmetic operations;
- Use mathematical functions with Excel.

CHAPTER I: TABLES WITH MS WORD

There are several ways to create tables in Word: by copying and pasting from Excel with or without a link (the link allows you to synchronize the data in the Word document with that in the Excel document), or by drawing the table directly in Word. You can also create an Excel table in your Word document, with all the Excel tools temporarily available to you!

You should choose Word to create a table if it contains complex graphic formatting: bulleted lists, custom tabs, numbered lists, first line indents, different formatting for different cells, or diagonal cell splitting. Word also offers a web layout.

However, you should choose Excel if you plan to insert complex calculations, statistical analyses, or diagrams into your table. Excel also provides advanced sorting and search functions.
If you insert a table into Word, it will initially be "standard," i.e., with the same number of cells per row and column. To transform it into an asymmetrical table, you will then need to merge or split certain cells. Even if your table is quite unusual, this may be the easiest way to proceed if you are just starting out.

You can also draw all the lines of the table with your mouse. In this case, it is a good idea to prepare a template on paper first.

I.1. CREATING A TABLE WITH MS WORD

To create a table with MS Word, follow these steps:

- Click in the document where you want to create a table.

- First method: on the **Insert** ribbon, click **Table**, then drag the mouse pointer to select the number of rows and columns you want.

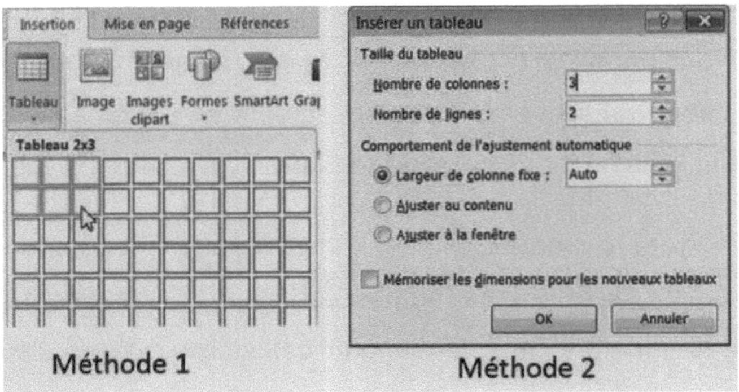

- Second method: on the **Insert** ribbon, click **Table**, **Insert Table**, then enter the appropriate values in the **Insert Table** dialog box.
- Get into the habit of displaying hidden elements so that you can see all the elements that make up the table (by clicking on ¶ on the **Home** ribbon), and preferably choose *Page* view.
- An empty table appears in the document, and in Word 2010, the *Table Tools* **Design** and **Layout** ribbons appear. They disappear as soon as you click outside the table.

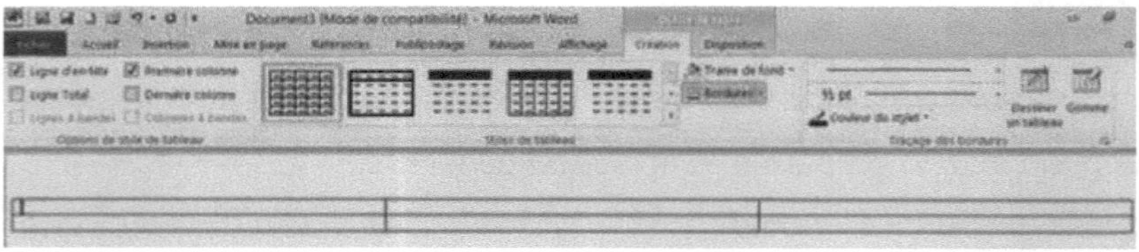

- The name of these contextual ribbons/tabs varies depending on your version of Word. In recent versions of Word such as Word 365 for Windows and macOS, they appear **in blue on the right side of the screen,** only when the pointer is in a table. These ribbons are called

Table Design and **Layout.** Please note that this is not the black **Layout** tab located between the **Design** tab and the **References** tab, but the blue **Layout** tab on the far right (*illustration below*).

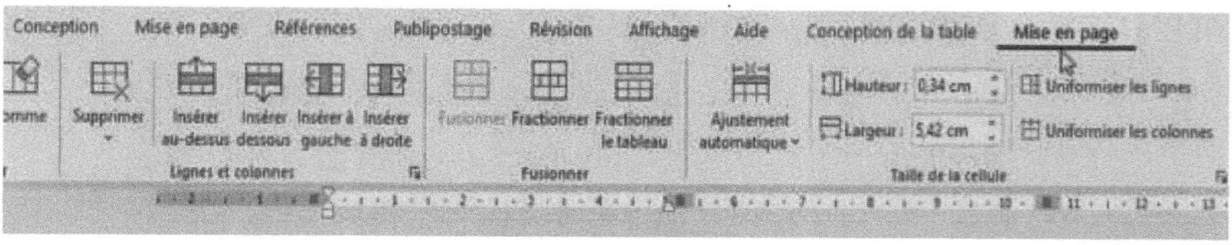

- As always with graphic elements, the style gallery in the center of the **Design** ribbon (*see above*) offers predefined table formats. Click on the triangle on the right to display all available templates and click on one of them if it meets your needs.

I.2. MANIPULATING A WORD TABLE

Once the table is displayed, it behaves like a graphic element. To resize, move, delete, etc., you need to know where to click and how. Let's start with the table's "strategic ."

CHARACTER MASK	ROLE
	Table selection and movement handle (appears in the upper left corner in Page view mode when the pointer is nearby).
	End of cell or line marker.
	Table resizing handle (in the lower left corner in Page view mode Page when the pointer is near proximity).

Since the table is a graphical element, it is important to know how to interpret the shape of the mouse pointer and where to position it for certain operations:

POINTER	WHERE TO POINT	ACTION
	On a line vertical	Click and drag to widen or reduce the width of a column.
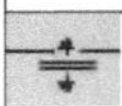	On a line horizontal	Click and drag to widen or reduce the height of a line.
	On the selection handle of the table (top left corner)	Click to select the entire table. Click and drag this handle to move the entire table within the document. Click right- to obtain table-related commands (see below)
	On the line top of a	Click to select the column.
	column	Click right to obtain the commands related to the table.
	In the margin , in opposite a line	Click to select the line. Click right to get the commands related to the table.
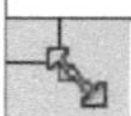	On the resize handle resize	Click and and to resize the table.

Almost all of these operations can be performed directly with the mouse, but if you are not very skilled with the mouse or are working in Draft mode, there are other ways to do them.

To begin with, you can use the Select menu on the left of the Layout ribbon to select the cell you clicked on, the column of the active cell, the row of the active cell, or the entire table:

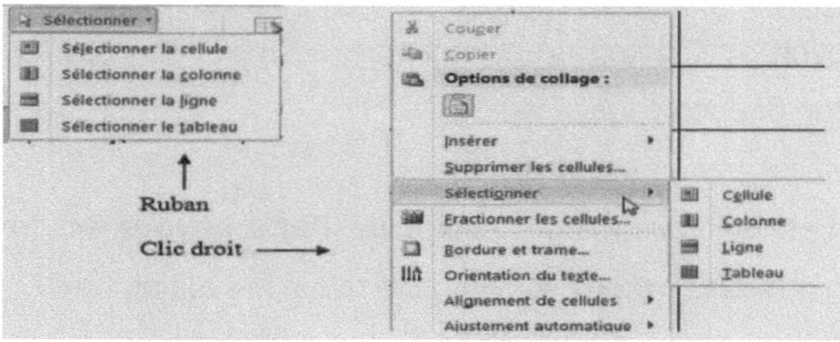

You can also right-click to access the same selection options (*see above*).

I.3. ALIGN AND SPLIT A WORD TABLE

Tables share some characteristics with other graphic elements in Word, such as page alignment options.

- Click **Properties** to the left of **the Layout** ribbon/blue **Page Layout** tab, then click an alignment option in the *Table Properties* dialog box:

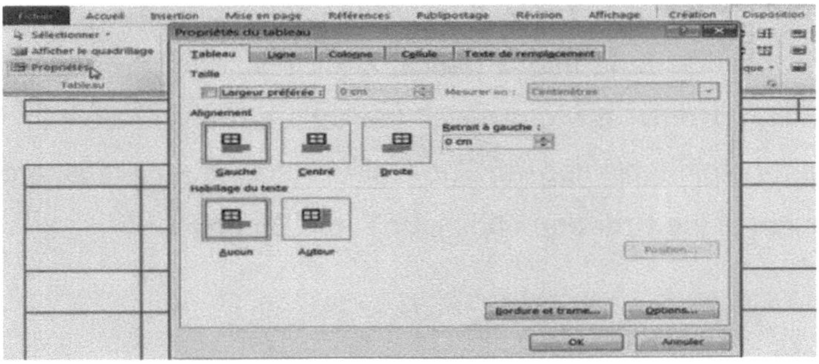

- Note that the *Text wrapping* section of the **Table** tab offers the **Around** option to frame the table with text (as with image).

- Splitting occurs naturally when the table continues on the next page, but you can force this separation by clicking in the first row of the second table and then **clicking Split Table** on the Layout ribbon/blue **Page Layout** tab.
- If the table "overflows" onto one or more pages, you can copy the header row to the top of each page...
- Click in the header row of the table.
- Click **Properties** on the **Lay**out ribbon/blue **Page Layout** tab (or right-click, **Table Properties**), then click the *Line* tab in the dialog box.
- Check the **Repeat at top of each page as header row** box.
- Of course, you will only be able to see the effect of this property in **Page** view.

I.4. DRAWING A TABLE "BY HAND" IN WORD

There is another way to draw a table, designed for more complex tables with cells of different heights or a variable number of columns per row, for example.

- On the **Insert** ribbon, click **Table**, then **Draw Table.**
- The mouse pointer turns into a pencil. Click and drag the mouse pointer diagonally to draw the outline of the table. The Creation and Layout ribbons for table tools appear. The tools for drawing the table are located to the right of the **Creation** ribbon (or **Table Design**).

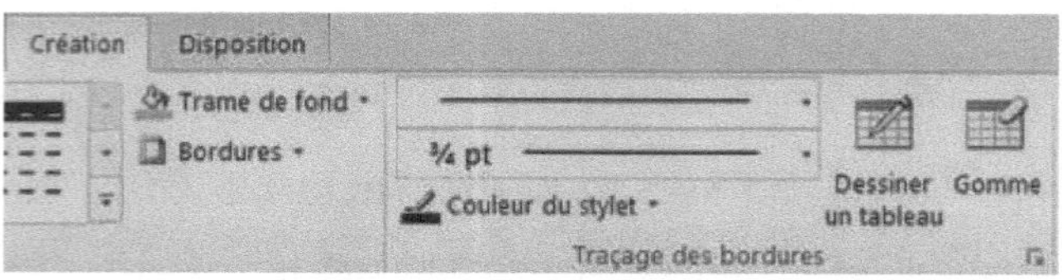

- Then draw the rows and columns inside the rectangle by clicking and dragging with the pencil.
- To delete a line or set of lines, click the

Eraser in the ribbon and then on the line you want to delete.

- Three lists allow you to change the line style, thickness, or color. The change will only apply to subsequent lines.
- **Tip:** if you have lost the pencil, simply click on **Draw a table** again in the **Creation** ribbon (or the blue **Layout** tab in Word 365).
- A drawn table behaves exactly like an inserted table, so you can apply all the techniques for filling and formatting it.

I.5. FORMATTING CELLS IN A WORD TABLE

To fill a table, simply click in the cells and enter your text. For character formatting, you have all the tools on **the Home** ribbon, just as when you enter text in the document. Here are the formatting options specific to tables.

- **Positioning text in a cell:** select the cells you want to format, then click one of the tools in the **Alignment** group on the **Layout** ribbon (or the blue **Layout** tab). In Word 2010, you can also right-click and select **Cell Alignment**. Take a close look at the icon; the design is fairly self-explanatory and represents the position of the text in the cell.

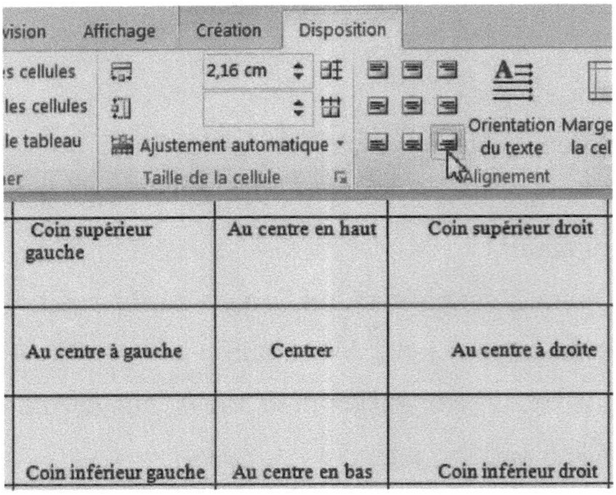

- **Orientation of text in the cell:** select the cell(s) concerned, then click on **Text Orientation** in the Layout ribbon/blue **Page Layout** tab (or right-click, **Text Orientation**). Click several times to switch between orientations. With each click, the left alignment icons change to reflect the new orientation.

•

- **Cell margins:** select the cell(s) concerned, then click on **Cell Margin** on the Layout ribbon/blue **Page Layout** tab. Enter the margin size in the dialog box that appears.
- **Note:** The text style in your cells has before and after spacing properties that already impose a "gap" between the lines of text and the top and bottom edges of the cell. If you specify top and bottom margins, you increase the initial gap.
- **Split or merge cells:** Sometimes you need to combine two cells into one or create several cells from one. First select the cell or cells you want to change. Then click **Merge Cells** or **Split Cells** on the **Layout** tab **in** the blue ribbon. You can also access these commands by right-clicking.

CHAPTER II: GRAPHIC OBJECTS IN MS WORD I.1.INSERTING GEOMETRIC SHAPES IN MS WORD

Geometric shapes allow you to enhance the presentation of your Word document and model concepts. s been updated over the years to offer a wider range of shapes: in addition to basic shapes (squares, triangles, arrows, etc.), you can now insert lines drawn with the mouse, curves, symbols , equation symbols, , flowchart elements, callouts, legends, various stars, banners, and more.

To insert geometric shapes in Word, simply follow these steps:

1. Click on the **Insert** tab.

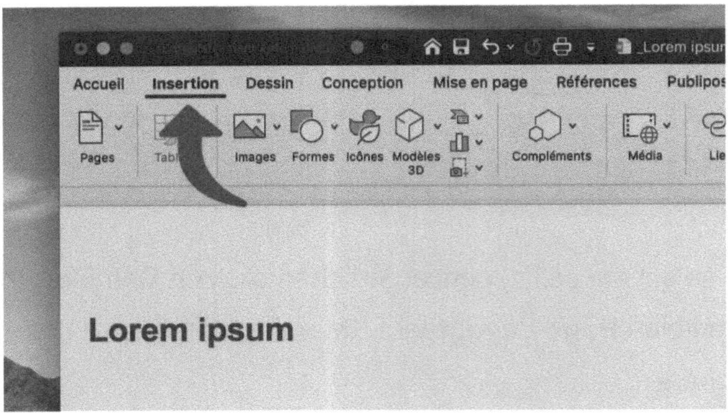

2. Click on the **Shapes** button.

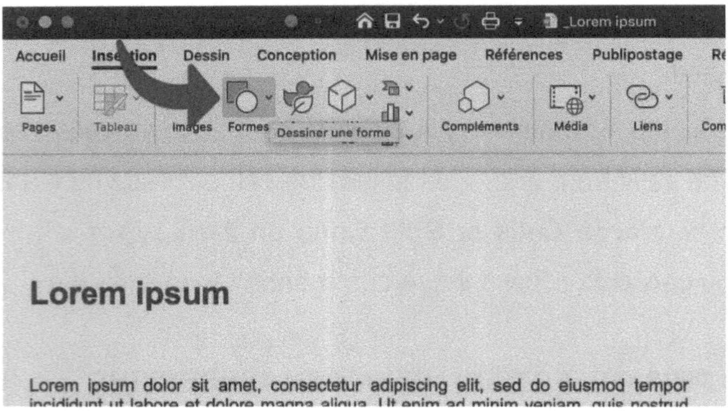

3. In the drop-down menu, select the **shape** you want.

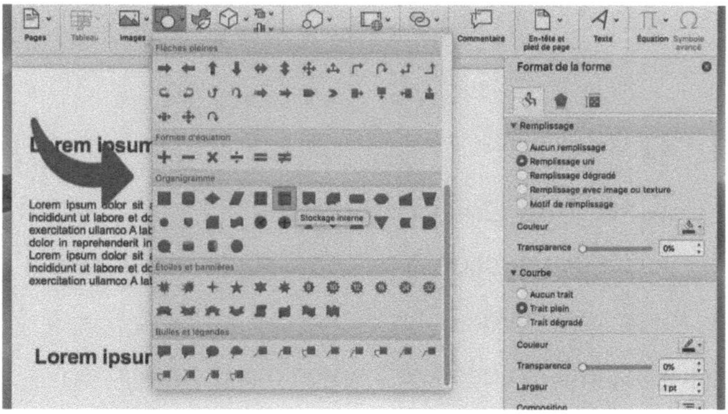

4. Click in the document where you want to insert the shape.

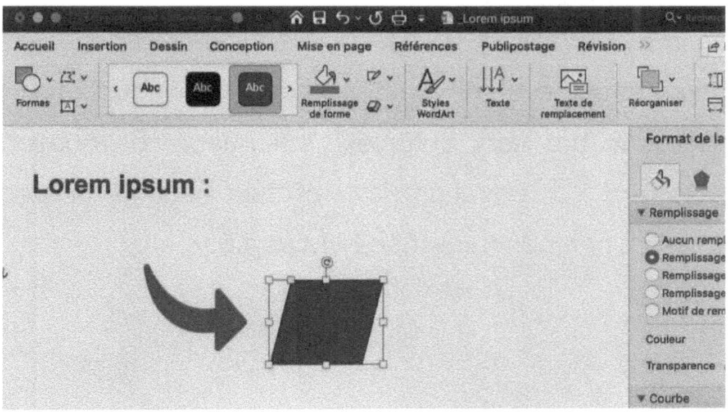

Once inserted, you can move the shape or change its appearance by right-clicking and selecting **Format Shape**. To add text to your shape, the most accurate way is to create a text box.

CHAPTER III: MATHEMATICAL SYMBOLS AND EQUATIONS

III.1.EQUATIONS

III.1.1. INSERTING AN EQUATION

Click on the arrow below the large "*Equations*" button

: You can then simply select an equation. You can also display the " Autres équations sur Office.com ." You will not be redirected to Office.com in your browser; it is just a list that is added, with even more equations:

If none of the equations in these two lists are suitable, you can click on " π Insérer une nouvelle équation " at the bottom of the list.

To set an average level in math and test the equations, I suggest a formula that is not very complex: the quadratic equation formula, root of an equation of the second degree ax2+bx+c=0ax2+bx+c=0 when b2+4ac>0b2+4ac>0:

$$x = \frac{-b\pm\sqrt{b^2-4ac}}{2a}$$

When you clicked on the equation, a new tab appeared: "*[Equation Tools] Design*." It is customary in this course to introduce the tabs, so we will do so here.

III.1.2. EQUATION TOOLS OR DESIGN

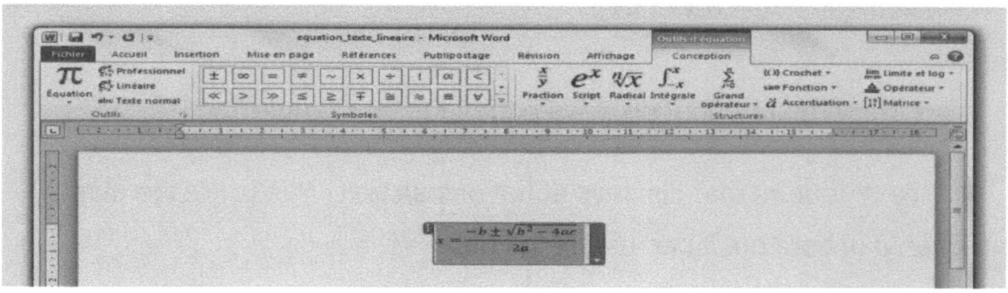

Note that there are only three groups:

Tools

The first group allows you to insert a new equation at the selected location. For example, if you selected the numerator and then clicked on insert equation, this new equation would become the numerator of the complete equation.

An example:

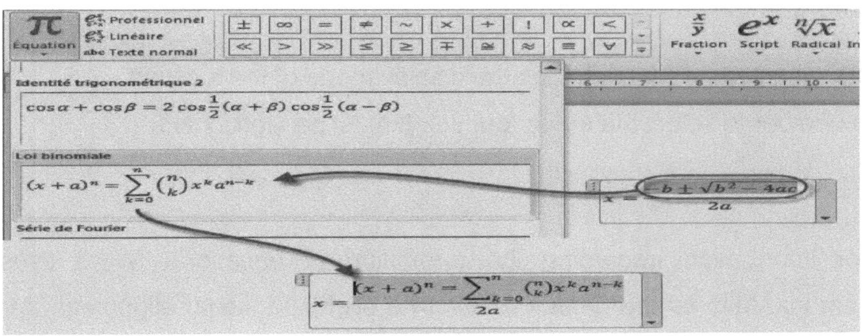

The other two functions allow you to place equations on two lines (the "/" symbol is used for fractions). The third function converts the equation to normal text and vice versa.

To summarize with a few examples:

- **Professional**: default feature for normal equation display - as we saw in the first test document

;

- **Linear**: feature that displays equations on a single line;

❖ **Text**: feature that displays equations as text. This is not the most suitable option, but it can be useful:

$$x = (-b \pm \surd(b\text{^}2 - 4ac))/2a$$

❖ **Linear text**: you can combine the two features. Click on "*Text*" and then on "*Linear*":

$$\mathrm{x}=\frac{\mathrm{-b}\pm\sqrt{\mathrm{b}^{2}\mathrm{-4ac}}}{\mathrm{2a}}$$

$$x = \frac{-b \pm \sqrt{b^2 - 4ac}}{2a}$$

NB: when you want to change the display mode of the function, remember to select the entire formula. It must be highlighted

. To do this, use the shortcut Ctrl +A .

For information, regarding the formatting of equations, Word uses Cambria italic as the default font with a slightly unusual alignment: if a line contains only an equation without text, it is centered; as soon as even a single space is added to the same line , it takes on the alignment of the text and switches to linear mode.

III.2. SYMBOLS

III.2.1. INSERTING SYMBOLS

To find a symbol, simply click on the "
Symbols" button, and a small menu will appear:

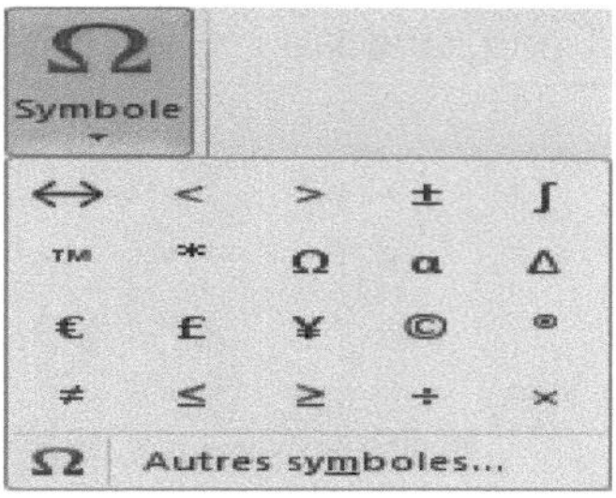

A small sample of symbols will appear in front of you. You can select one of them, and it will automatically appear in your document at the cursor location. You can also select "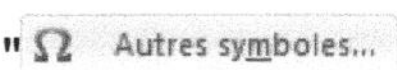

" to open this window:

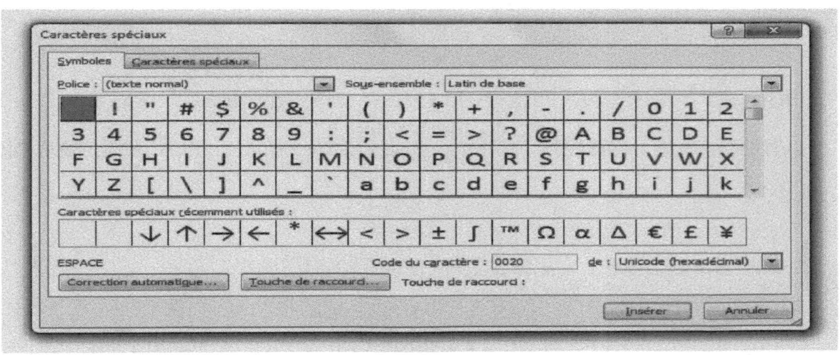

From there, a long list of characters is available.

All categories (*Basic Latin*, *Latin-1 Supplement*, *Latin Extended A/B*, etc.) are combined, and you can insert the symbol you want, in the font you want.

Note that recently used characters are easier to access.

Here, as in the quick menu, click on the desired character and then on "*Insert.*" The character is inserted into the document, but the window remains open so you can add other symbols.

Regarding "*Special characters,*" "*AutoCorrect,*" and "*Shortcut keys,*" we will cover the first two in a chapter in the last part, and we covered the third in a chapter in the first part.

III.2.2. LIST ICONS

Another use for symbols is in bulleted lists.

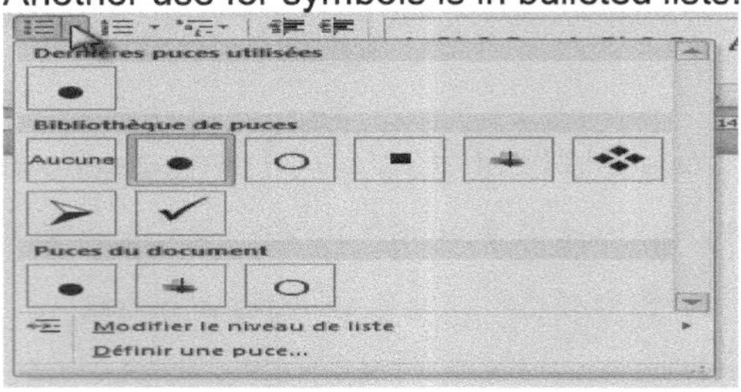

When we looked at bulleted lists, remember, we saw that it was possible to use a symbol as a bullet by clicking on "*Define a bullet...*" and then on "*Symbol*":

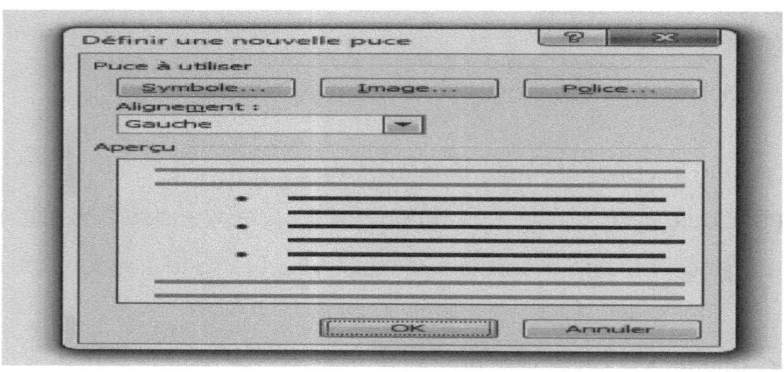

CHAPTER IV: MICROSOFT EXCEL SPREADSHEET INTERFACE

IV.1. SPREADSHEET

Microsoft Excel is the spreadsheet program in the *Microsoft Office* suite. To launch it, simply click on the appropriate icon in your *Start* menu (in Windows) or click on an Excel file (with the extension *.xls*).

An Excel document is called **a workbook** and contains one or more worksheets, which appear as tabs at the bottom of the page.

IV.1.1. INTERFACE OVERVIEW

The Microsoft Excel interface is shown below:

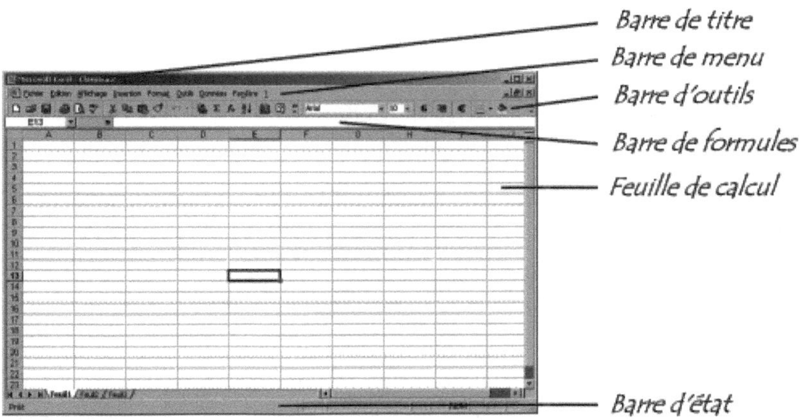

It consists of various elements:

1. **A title bar** showing the name of the application and the name of the open workbook
2. **A menu bar** providing access to the various spreadsheet functions

3. **A toolbar** with icons providing direct access to the main features. It is worth noting that this bar can be customized to allow you to add shortcuts to the features you use most often

4. **A formula bar** showing the address of the selected cell and its contents. The formula bar allows you to enter data to be inserted into cells

5. **The worksheet** is the key element of the spreadsheet; it is the table containing all the cells. At the bottom of the displayed worksheet are tabs that allow you to switch between worksheets.

6. **The status bar** provides information about actions to be taken or actions in . By default, the message *"Ready"* is displayed in the status bar.

IV.2. CELLS

Cell: A cell is the intersection of a row (horizontal) and a column (vertical).

- From a computer perspective, a cell is a variable that has a name and contains a value.

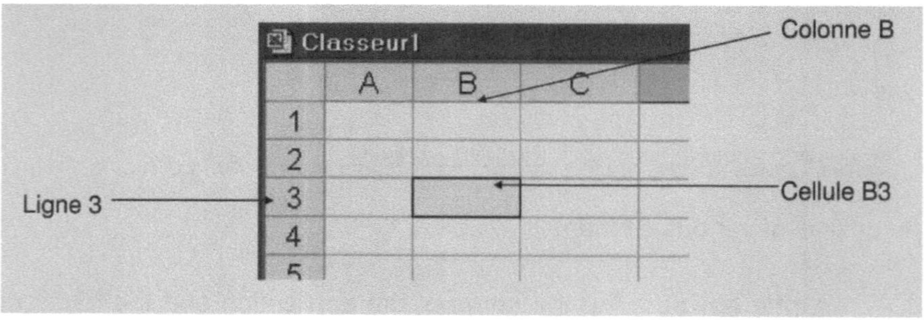

IV.3. TOOLBARS

You can access it from the File tab or the Home tab using the up arrow.

It contains buttons for the most frequently used operations. Their keyboard shortcuts are Alt, num, where num is the location of the button in the toolbar. For example, for the first button, the shortcut is Alt, 1. Remember to use the Shift key if you are using the alphanumeric keypad.

By default, you will find the "Save," "Undo," "Repeat," and "Customize Toolbar" buttons. The first buttons are of little interest to us since we already have the Ctrl +S, Ctrl +Z, and Ctrl +Y commands. To display other buttons, open the "Customize Toolbar" button by pressing Space or Enter. A number of commands are available. Press Space to confirm, which will close the menu.

If you select "More commands" from this list, you will open the "Word Options" dialog box under "Quick Access Toolbar." Press Tab to scroll through the list of commands.

Select "Paragraph Settings." Move to this item in the list. It is now selected. Press Tab twice to select the "Add" button, then press Space to confirm. "Paragraph Settings" now appears in the list of available buttons. You can even choose its location by tabbing to the "Move Up" and "Move Down" buttons. Tab to the OK button and press Enter until it is in the desired position. Click the "OK" button to close the dialog box. The "Paragraph settings" button is now in the quick access toolbar. If you placed it in the first position, simply press Alt, 1 to open the Paragraph dialog box.

IV.4. TABS

Since Office 2007, traditional menus have been replaced by a horizontal area called **a ribbon**. This area consists of:

- the **tab bar**, containing a button where NVDA says "File tab button," followed by a series of tabs. It ends with an edit area called "Tell us what you want to do."
- Below this is the **lower ribbon**, where control elements (buttons, checkboxes, lists, etc.) are arranged in **groups**. NVDA s announces "grouping." These groups depend on the selected tab. Some of the elements, such as shared buttons or drop-down buttons, open context menus.
- Above is the **Quick Access** Toolbar.

You can access the tab bar by pressing Alt, then the bottom ribbon by pressing Tab or the down arrow or Ctrl + right arrow, or the quick access toolbar by pressing Shift + Tab or Ctrl + left arrow. The tab selected by default when you press Alt is Home.

In the tab bar, you can move using the right and left arrows.

Within the bottom ribbon, use Tab rather than the right and left arrows, as the items are not always arranged in a linear fashion. Ctrl + right and left arrows allow you to move from group to group, which limits the number of tabs. In total, pressing Ctrl + right arrow performs the following loop: group 1, subsequent groups, "File tab" button, first button on the quick toolbar, return to tabs. Ctrl + left arrow performs the reverse loop.

NOTES.

- For keyboard shortcuts relating to the ribbon, press the keys **in succession** rather than simultaneously, hence the notation with commas between the keys, for example Alt, F, W to reopen a Word document. The numbers in the commands can be entered using either the numeric keypad or the alphanumeric keypad. With the alphanumeric keypad, the Shift key must be pressed.

- Keyboard shortcuts are displayed each time an item is selected.
- Traditional commands, such as F12, remain available.

The basic tabs are: **Home, Insert, Create, Page Layout, References, Mailings, Review, and View.**

- The **Home** tab, opened by Alt, L, is one of the most important. Here you will find the Clipboard, Font, Paragraph, Style, and Editing groups (which contains the Find, Replace, and Select options).
- The **Insert** tab, opened by Alt, S, contains the Tables group, among others.
- The **Layout** tab, opened by Alt, P, contains the Page Setup and Paragraph groups (indentation and spacing), among others.
- The **Create, References**, **Mailings**, **Review**, and **View** tabs are only used for creating complex documents.

Tabs can be added depending on the task being performed. These are called "**contextual tabs**." For example, if the cursor is in a table, two tabs are added to the tab bar.

Each group consists of two overlapping parts: the upper part contains the control elements. The lower part contains the name of the group and sometimes a button. These buttons are important because they open dialog boxes that are almost identical to those found in Word 2003, for example for fonts, paragraphs, styles, etc. If a button is present, you can reach it with the Down Arrow. NVDA will say the name of the group and the keyboard shortcut, for example, "Office Clipboard, Alt button, L, EN." You can then move to the next or previous button using the right or left arrow keys, which allows you to move quickly through the lower ribbon. If there is no button, NVDA will not access this lower section.

CHAPTER V: FORMULAS AND ARITHMETIC OPERATORS

V.1. ARITHMETIC OPERATORS (PRIORITIES, CALCULATION ERRORS WITH MS WORD)

These allow you to perform basic mathematical operations.

- addition: + ;
- subtraction: -
- multiplication: *;
- division: /
- percentage: %;
- exponent: ^.

It is important to pay attention to the priorities of the operators, which are the same as in mathematics. In the example below, the results in D1 and D2 are different, giving 18.25 and 0.517.

V.1.1. PRIORITY

When multiple operations occur in an expression, each part is evaluated and resolved in a predetermined order called operator precedence.
When expressions contain operators from multiple categories, arithmetic operators are evaluated first, followed by comparison operators and logical operators.
Comparison operators all have equal priority; that is, they are evaluated in the order in which they appear from left to right.

Arithmetic and logical operators are evaluated in the following order of priority:

Arithmetic	Comparison	Logical
Exponentiation (^)	Equality (=)	**Not**
Negation (-)	Inequality (< >)	**And**
Multiplication and division (*, /)	Less than (<)	**Or**
Division of an integer (\)	Greater than (>)	**Xor**
Modulus arithmetic (Mod)	Less than or equal to (< =)	**Eqv**
Addition and subtraction (+, -)	Greater than or equal to (> =)	**Imp**
String concatenation (&)	**Like, is**	

When both multiplication and division occur in an expression, the operations are evaluated from left to right. When both addition and subtraction occur in an expression, the operations are evaluated from left to right.

Parentheses can be used to override the order of precedence and force certain parts of an expression to be evaluated before others. Operations within parentheses are always performed before those outside the parentheses. However, the precedence of operators is preserved within parentheses.

The string concatenation operator & is not an arithmetic operator, but in terms of priority, it follows all arithmetic operators and precedes all comparison operators.

The **Like** operator has the same priority as all comparison operators, but is actually a special character operator.

The **Is** operator is an object reference comparison operator. It does not compare objects or their values; it only determines whether two object references refer to the same object.

The order of decreasing priority.

- - negation (as in -1);
- %: percentage;
- ^ : exponent;
- * and / : multiplication and division;
- + and – : addition and subtraction;
- &: concatenation of two text strings;
- =<><= >=<> : comparison.

Given the formula =5+2*3, the result is 11 (the expression 2*3 is evaluated first because of operator precedence).

Given the formula = (5+2)*3, the result is 21 (the expression 5+2 is evaluated first because of the parentheses).

CHAPTER VI: MATHEMATICAL FUNCTIONS WITH MS EXCEL

VI.1. SUM

The Excel **SUM** function calculates the sum of a series of values.

Usage: =SUM(values)

EXAMPLE

The SUM function has its own shortcut, so you don't need to search for SUM in the list of functions.

Click on the cell that will contain the sum, then click on the Auto s symbol "AutoSum" ():

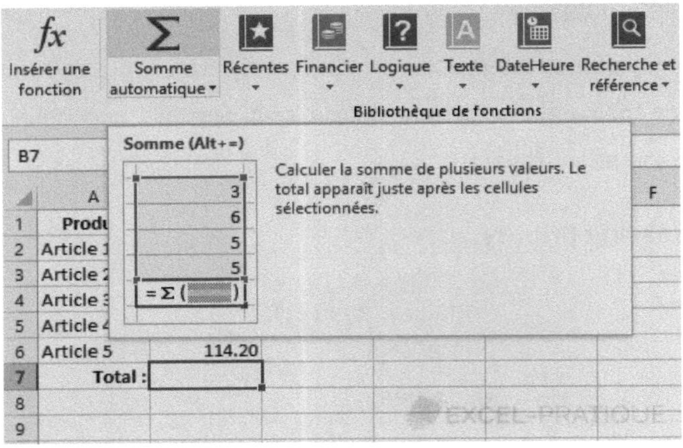

A list of values is automatically preselected.

If it is correct, press Enter; if not, make another selection and press Enter.

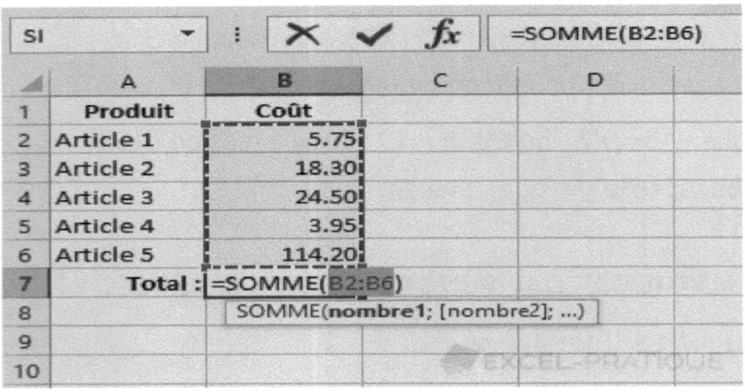

The sum is calculated:

B7 =SOMME(B2:B6)

	A	B	C	D
1	Produit	Coût		
2	Article 1	5.75		
3	Article 2	18.30		
4	Article 3	24.50		
5	Article 4	3.95		
6	Article 5	114.20		
7	Total :	166.70		
8				
9				
10				

VI.2. PRODUCT

The **PRODUCT** function returns the product of a set of arguments. This function is limited to 30 arguments.

Its structure is:

=PRODUCT (*number1*; *number2*; *[number3]*; ...)

Where *number1, number2, [number3], etc.* correspond to the numbers whose product is sought.

EXAMPLE:

Fonction Produit

Nombre 1	Nombre 2	Nombre 3	Formule (Fonction PRODUIT)	Résultat (Fonction PRODUIT)
18	12	16	=PRODUIT(B5;C5;D5)	3456
25	15	35	=PRODUIT(B6;C6;D6)	13125
3	18	14	=PRODUIT(B7;C7;D7)	756
8	17	9	=PRODUIT(B8;C8;D8)	1224

VI.3. QUOTIENT

The QUOTIENT function returns the integer part of a division, the first argument is the numerator and the second argument is the denominator. Its structure is:

=QUOTIENT(*numerator; denominator*) **Example:**

Fonction Quotient

		Formule mathématique		Fonction Quotient	
Numérateur	Dénominateur	Équation	Résultat	Formule	Résultat
22	10	= 22 / 10	2,2	=QUOTIENT(B5;C5)	2
417	15	= 417 / 15	27,8	=QUOTIENT(B6;C6)	27
3	3	= 3 / 3	1	=QUOTIENT(B7;C7)	1
7	3	= 7 / 3	2,3333333	=QUOTIENT(B8;C8)	2

VI.4. POWER

You can square a number in Excel using the power function, which is represented by the caret symbol ^. Use the formula **=N^2**, where N is either a number or the value of the cell you want to square. This formula can be used multiple times in a worksheet.

VI.4.1. ENTER A NUMBER IN ITS OWN CELL

Proceed as follows:

1. Click in a cell in your spreadsheet.
2. Type **=N^2** in the cell, where N is the number you want to square. For example, to insert the square of 5 in cell A1, type **=5^2** in the cell.

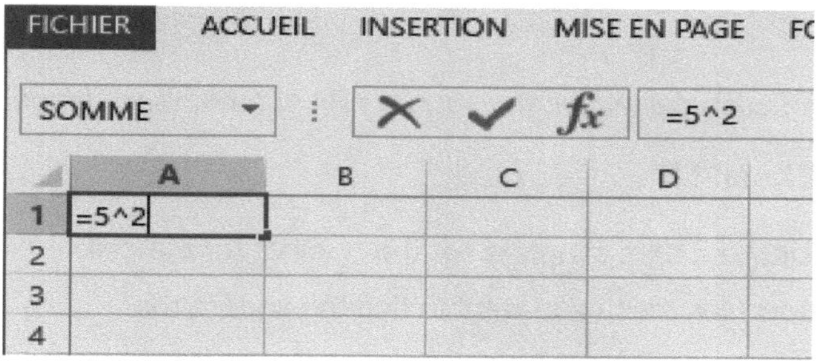

3. Press Enter to display the result.

Note: You can also click in another cell to display the squared result.

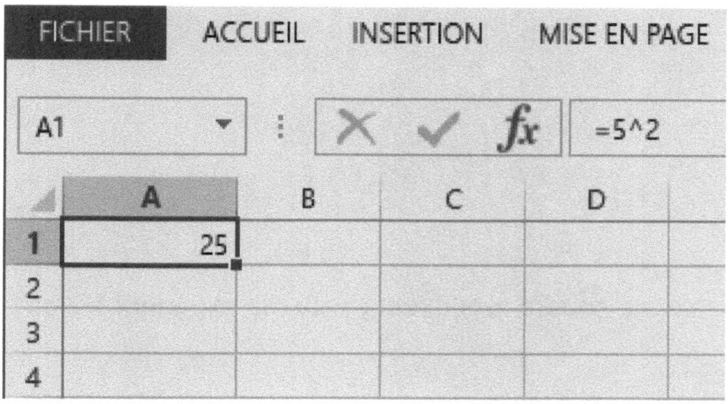

VI.4.2. SQUARING A NUMBER IN A DIFFERENT CELL

Proceed as follows:

1. Click inside a cell and type the number you want to square.
2. Select another empty cell in the worksheet.
3. Type **=N^2** in the empty cell, where N is a cell reference that contains the numerical value you want to square. For example, to display the square of the value in cell A1 , type **=A1^2** in cell B1.

VI.5. ROOT

The Excel **ROOT** function calculates the square root of a number. Usage:

=SQRT(number) EXAMPLE

Select the ROOT function, then simply enter the number (or the cell containing the number) for which you want to find the square root:

=SQUARE ROOT(B1)

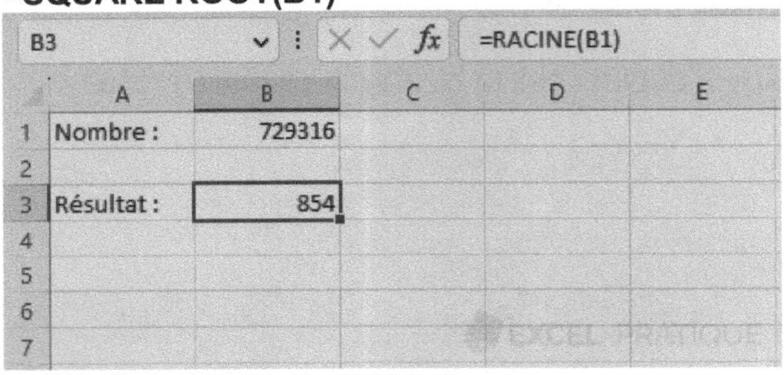

ALTERNATIVE

You can also calculate the square root directly with the exponent 1/2 or 0.5:

=B1^0.5

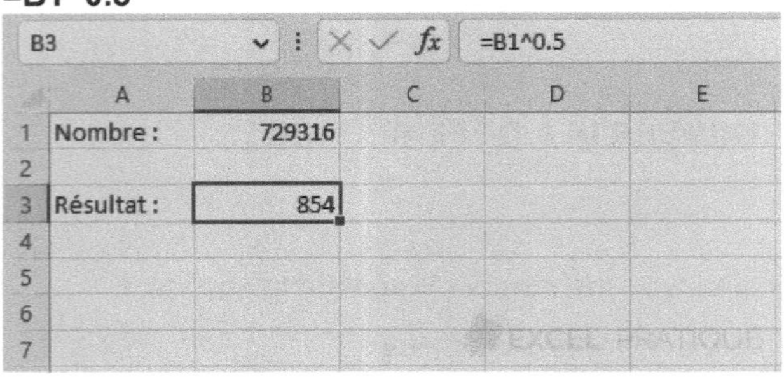

Or, for example, with 1 / 3 for the cube root:

=B1^(1/3)

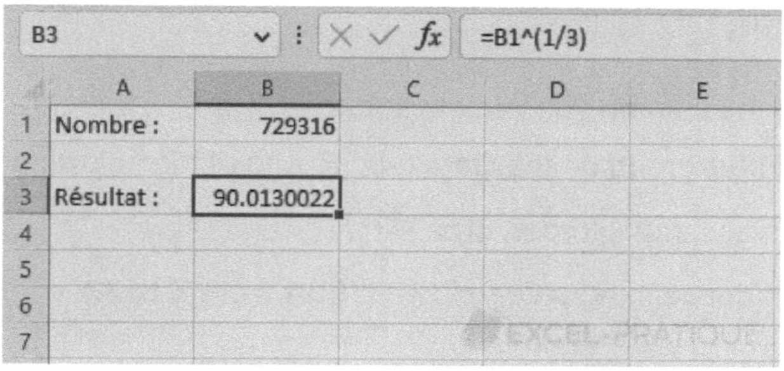

CHAPTER VII: DATA MANAGEMENT AND ORGANIZATION

VII.1. SORT

Sorting data is an integral part of data analysis. For example, you may need to sort a list of names alphabetically, compile a list of product inventory levels from highest to lowest, or arrange rows by color or icon. Sorting data allows you to quickly view and understand your data, organize and search for specific data, and ultimately make decisions more effectively.

You can sort data based on text (A to Z or Z to A), numbers (smallest to largest or largest to smallest), and dates and times (oldest to newest and newest to oldest) in one or more columns. You can also sort based on a custom list that you create (for example, Large, Medium, and Small) or based on formatting, including cell color, font color, or icon set. To find the lowest or highest values in a range of cells or in a table (such as the top 10 r the lowest 5 sales volumes), use the AutoFilter feature or conditional formatting.

VII.1.1. TEXT SORTING

1. Select a cell in the column you want to sort.
2. In the **Sort & Filter** group on the **Data** tab, do one of the following:

- **To** sort in ascending order, click " ."
- To sort in descending order, click (**Sort from Z to A**).

NOTES: POTENTIAL PROBLEMS

- Make sure all data is stored as text. If the column you want to sort contains numbers stored as numbers and numbers stored as text, you must format them all as numbers or text. If you do not apply this format, numbers stored as numbers are sorted before numbers stored as text. To format all selected data as text, press Ctrl+1 to launch the Format Cells dialog box, then click the Number tab, and under Category, click General, Number, or Text.
- Remove spaces on the left In some cases, data imported from another application is preceded by spaces. Remove these spaces before sorting the data. You can do this manually, or you can use the TRIM function.

VII.1.2. SORT NUMBERS

1. Select a cell in the column you want to sort.
2. In the **Sort & Filter** group on the **Data** tab, do one of the following:

- To sort in ascending order, click Sort (**Sort from smallest to largest**).
- To sort in descending order, click **Sort Largest to Smallest**.

NOTES: POTENTIAL PROBLEM

❖ **Verify that all numbers are stored as numbers** If the result is not what you expected, the column may contain numbers stored as text, not numbers. For example, negative numbers imported from some accounting systems or a number preceded by an apostrophe (') are stored as text

VII.1.3. SORTING DATES AND TIMES

1. Select a cell in the column you want to sort.
2. In the **Sort & Filter** group on the **Home** tab, do one of the following:

❖ To sort from the oldest date or time to the most recent, click "**Sort from oldest to most recent**."

❖ To sort from the most recent date or time to the oldest, click **Sort from Newest to Oldest**.

NOTES: POTENTIAL PROBLEM

❖ **Check that dates and times are stored as dates and times** If the result is not what you expected, the column may contain dates or times stored as text in the " " instead of being stored as dates or times. In order for Excel to sort by dates and times, all dates and times in a column must be stored as date and time serial numbers. If Excel cannot recognize a value as a date or time, it may be stored as text.

❖ To sort by days of the week, format the cells so that they display the days of the week. To sort by days of the week regardless of the date, convert the dates to text using the TEXT function. However, be aware that this function returns a text value and sorting is performed based on alphanumeric data.

VII.1.4. SORTING BY CRITERIA OTHER THAN A COLUMN OR ROW

You can sort across multiple columns or rows when you have data that you want to group by the same value in a column or row, and then sort the data in another column or row within that group of equal values. For example, if a spreadsheet has columns Department and Employee, you can sort by the Department column first (to group all employees in the same department), then sort by the Employee column (to sort names alphabetically within each department). You can sort up to 64 columns.

NOTE: For best results, the range of cells you sort should have column headings.

1. Select any cell in the data range.

	A	B
1	Nom	Service
2	Pruitt, Barbara	Ventes
3	Fife, Grant	Marketing
4	Snook, Anthony	Opérations
5	Horn, Frances	Finances
6	Barrett, Alicia	Crédit
7	Larson, Lynn	Paie
8	Brown, Charity	Ventes
9	Bartels, Freddy	Marketing
10	Harding, Marcella	Opérations
11	Reuter, Randall	Finances
12	McDaniel, Evelyn	Crédit

2. In the **Sort & Filter** group on the **Data** tab, click **Sort**.

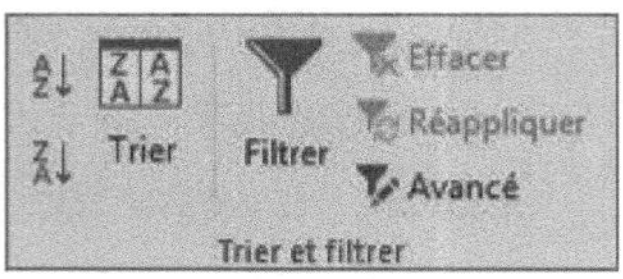

3. In the **Sort** dialog box, under **Column**, in the **Sort by** box, select the first column to sort.

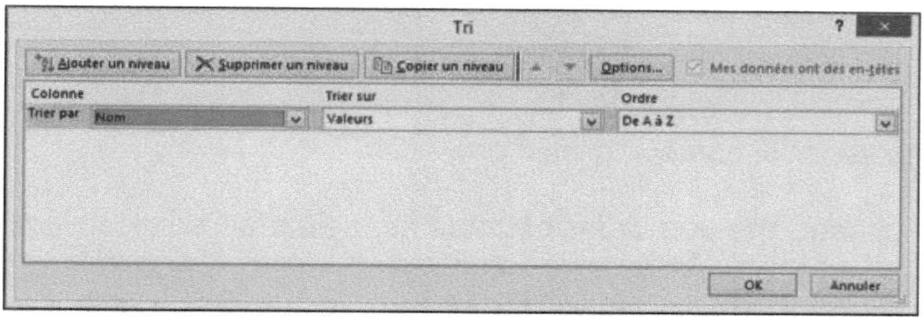

4. Under **Sort by**, select the sort type. Do one of the following:

❖ To sort by text, a number, or a date and time, select **Values**.

❖ To sort by formatting, select **Cell Color** , **Font Color**, or **Cell Icon**.

5. Under **Order**, select how you want the sorting to be done. Do one of the following:

❖ For text values, select **A to Z** or **Z to A**.

❖ For numeric values, select **Smallest to Largest** or **Largest to Smallest**.

❖ For date or time values, select **Oldest to Newest** or **Newest to Oldest**.

❖ To sort according to a custom list, select **Custom List**.

6. To add a column to sort, click **Add Level**, then repeat steps three through five.

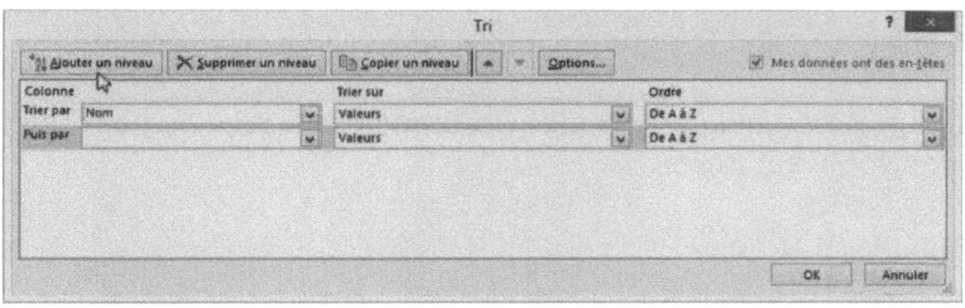

7. To copy a column to sort, select the entry, then click **Copy Level**.

8. To delete a column to sort, select the entry, then click **Delete a level**.

NOTE: The list must contain at least one entry.

9. To change the sort order of columns, select an entry, select " ," and then click the **Up** or **Down** arrow next to the **Options** button to change the order. Entries higher in the list are sorted before entries lower in the list.

VII.1.6. SORT BY CELL COLOR, FONT, OR ICON

If you have applied manual or conditional formatting to a range of cells or a table column by cell color or font, you can sort by those colors. You can also sort by a set of icons that you created with conditional formatting.

1. Select a cell in the column you want to sort.
2. In the **Sort & Filter** group on the **Data** tab, click **Sort**.

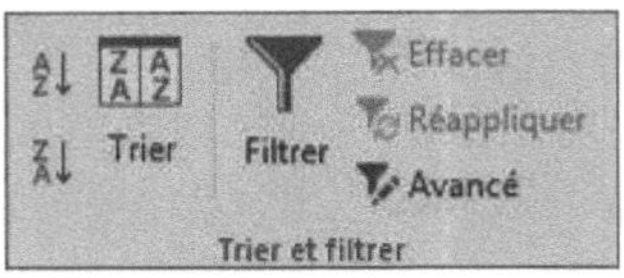

3. In the **Sort** dialog box, under **Column**, in the **Sort by** box, select the column you want to sort.

4.

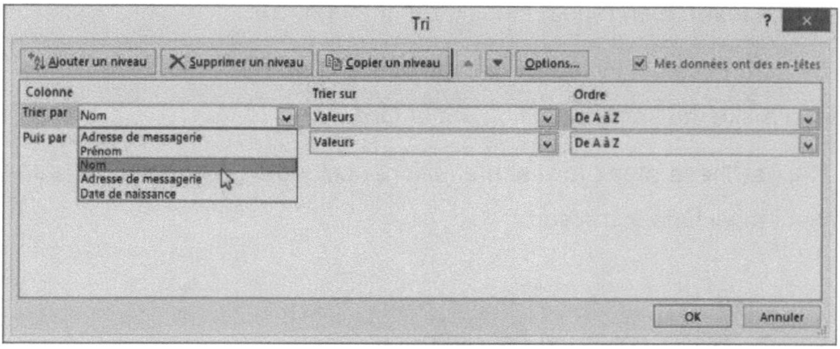

5. Under **Sort on**, select **Cell Color**, **Cell Font**, or **Cell Icon**.

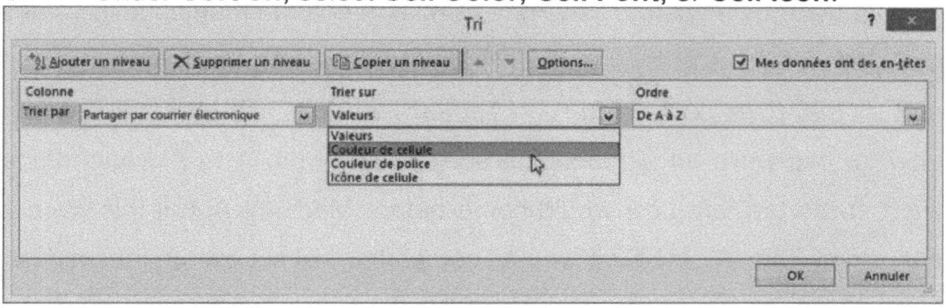

6. Under **Order**, click the arrow next to the button and, depending on the format type, select a cell color, font color, or cell icon.

7. Then select how you want the sorting to be done. Do one of the following:

- To move the cell color, font color, or icon up or to the left, select **Top** for column sorting and **Left** for row sorting.
- To move the cell color, font color, or icon down or to the right, select **Down** for column sorting and **Right** for row sorting.

Note: There is no default sort order for cell color, font color, or icon. You must define the order for each sort operation.

8. To specify the next cell color, font color, or icon to sort by, click **Add a level**, then repeat steps three through five.

Be sure to select the same column in the **Then by**

and make the same selection under **Order**.

Repeat these steps for each additional cell color, font color, or icon you want to include in the sort.

VII.1.7. SORT BY CUSTOM LIST

You can sort by a custom list. For example, a column may contain values that you want to sort by, such as High, Medium, and Low. How can you sort so that rows containing High appear first, followed by Medium, then Low? If this were an alphabetical sort, sorting from A to Z would place High at the top, but Low would come before Medium. And if this were a sort from Z to A, Medium would come first, with Low in the middle. Regardless of the order, you want Medium to always appear in the middle. By creating your own list, you can work around this problem.

1. You can also create a custom list:

a. In a range of cells, enter the values that will be used as sorting criteria, in the desired order, from top to bottom, as in this example .

	A
1	Haute
2	Moyenne
3	Faible

b. Select the range you just entered. Using the previous

example, select cells A1:A3.

c. Go to **File> Options> Advanced> General> Edit Custom Lists**, then in the **Custom Lists** dialog box, click **Import**, then **OK** twice.

NOTES:

❖ You can only create a custom list based on a value (text, numeric, or date and time). You cannot create a custom list based on formatting (cell color, font color, or icon).

❖ A custom list can have a maximum of 255 characters and must not start with a number.

2. Select a cell in the column you want to sort.

3. In the **Sort & Filter** group on the **Data** tab, click **Sort**.

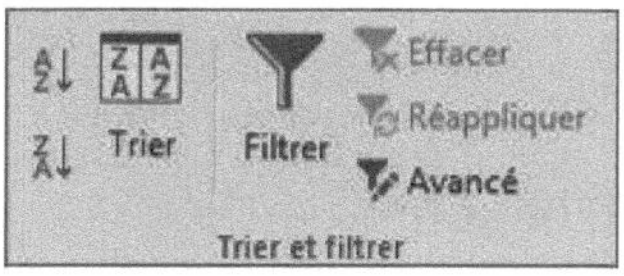

4. In the **Sort** dialog box, under **Column**, in the **Sort by** or **Then by** box, select the column you want to sort according to a custom list.

5. Under **Order**, select **Custom List**.

6. In the **Custom Lists** dialog box, select the list you want. Using the custom list you created in the previous example, click **High, Medium, Low**.

7. Click **OK**.

VII.1.8. SORT BY CASE

- In the **Sort & Filter** group, on the **Data** tab, click **Sort**.

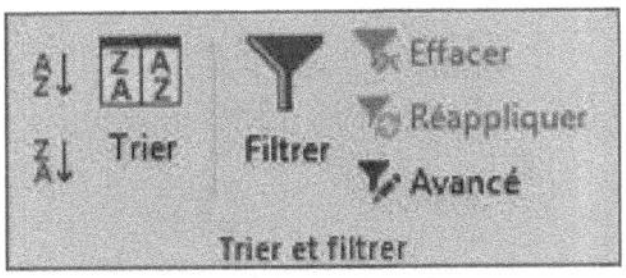

- In the **Sort by** box, click **Options**.

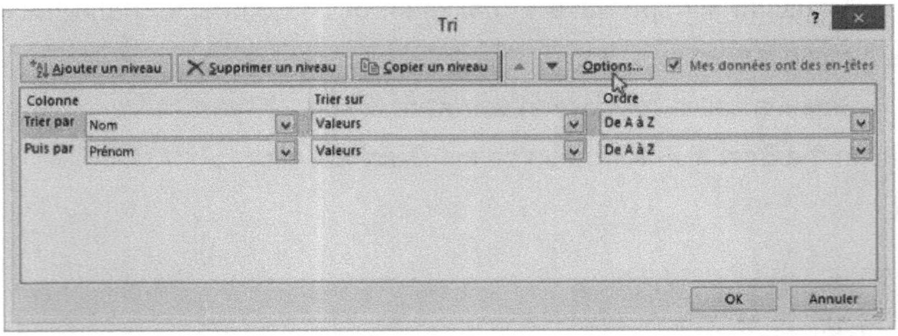

- In the **Sort Options** dialog box, select **Match case** .

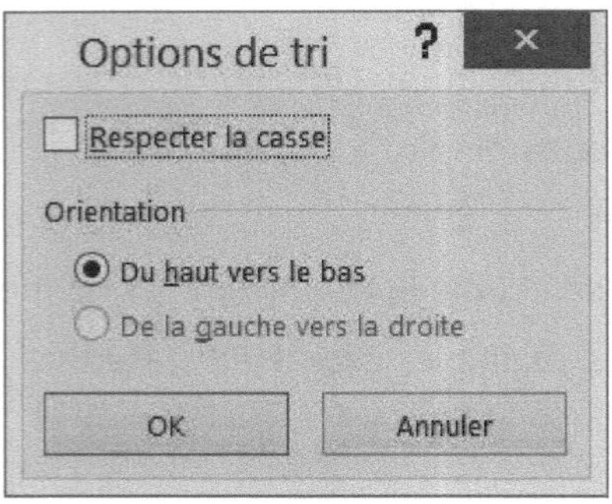

- Click **OK** twice.

VII.1.9. SORTING A RANGE WITHIN A LARGER RANGE

Note: It is possible to sort a range within a range, although this is not recommended because the result separates the sorted range from its original data. If you were to sort the following data as displayed, the selected employees would be associated with different departments than they were before.

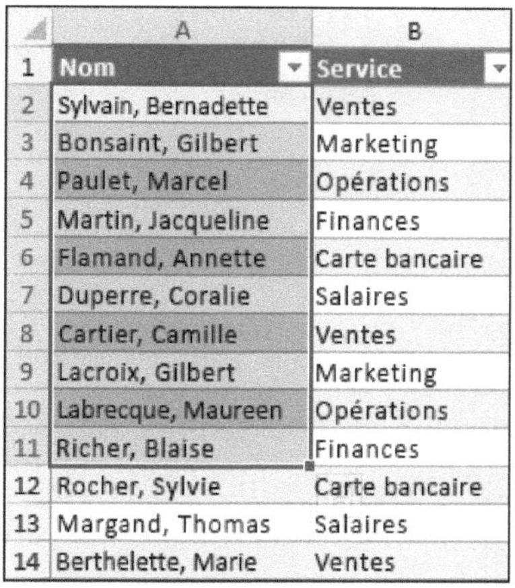

	A	B
1	Nom	Service
2	Sylvain, Bernadette	Ventes
3	Bonsaint, Gilbert	Marketing
4	Paulet, Marcel	Opérations
5	Martin, Jacqueline	Finances
6	Flamand, Annette	Carte bancaire
7	Duperre, Coralie	Salaires
8	Cartier, Camille	Ventes
9	Lacroix, Gilbert	Marketing
10	Labrecque, Maureen	Opérations
11	Richer, Blaise	Finances
12	Rocher, Sylvie	Carte bancaire
13	Margand, Thomas	Salaires
14	Berthelette, Marie	Ventes

Fortunately, Excel will notify you if it detects that you are about to try this:

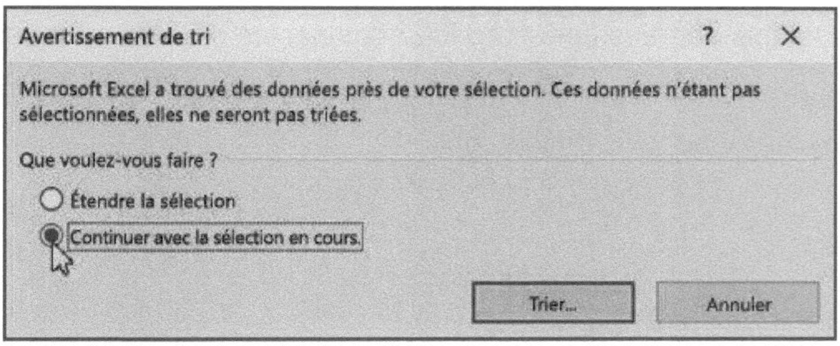

If you did not intend to apply this sort, press the **Expand Selection** option, otherwise select **Continue with Current Selection**.

If you did not get the results you expected, click **Cancel**

.

Note: You cannot apply this type of sorting in a table

VII.2. FILTERING DATA WITH MS EXCEL

In Excel, the *filter* function allows you to filter a range of data based on one or more defined criteria. These filters require specific formulas (or functions), but the basic patterns remain the same each time. The formulas you will need to know are as follows:

- =FILTER(table; criterion),
- =FILTER(table;(criterion1)*(criterion2)),
- =FILTER(table;(criterion1)+(criterion2)),
- =FILTER(table; criterion; "if no results").

Once put into practice, these models are easy to understand. At , we offer five examples to help you understand everything about the Excel *filter* function.

VII.2.1. CREATING AN EXCEL FILTER FOR A VALUE

The purpose of this first example is to filter companies that sell at least 8,000 units of products from all the data in the table on the left and obtain the filtered results in the table on the right.

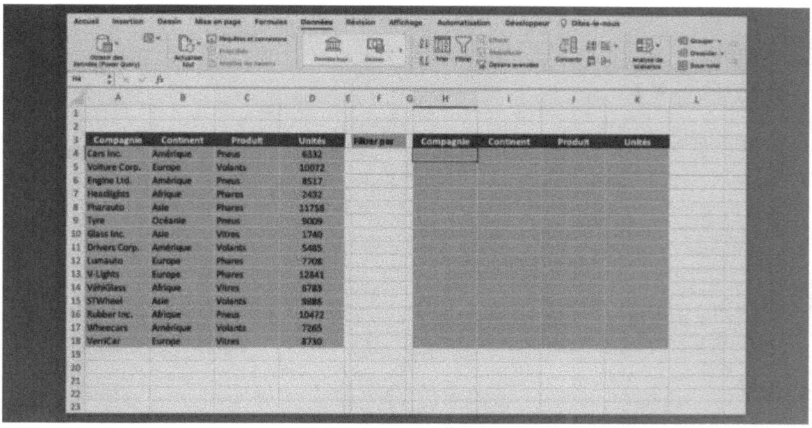

Here is the data table that we will use throughout this section.

To set up this filter, you must first select the cell (in our case, cell H4) that will contain the filter results . For , y , enter . For the , enter the formula: . This is the following : *=FILTER(A4:D18;D4:D18>=8000)*. How to understand it:

❖ *A4:D18* corresponds to the range taken into account in the operation, in this case our entire table.

❖ *D4:D18* corresponds to the range where the filter criterion must be applied, i.e. our product units,

❖ *>=8000* corresponds to the condition; we only want to keep companies that sell 8,000 units or more.

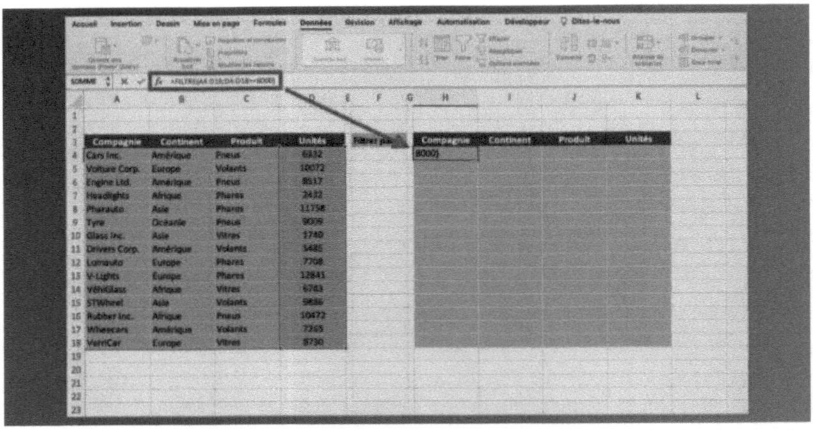

Excel highlights the elements entered in the formula in the table.

All you have to do is press *Enter* to validate the filter and see the results displayed. Here, we have a table of companies that sell more than 8,000 units of any product.

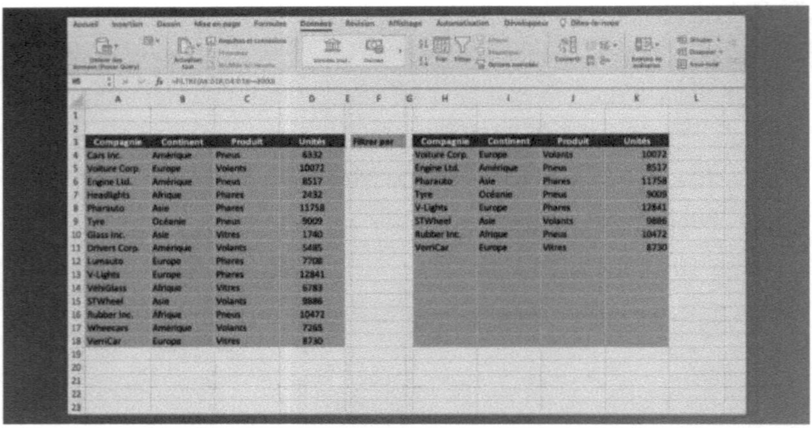

Once the formula has been entered correctly, the filter is applied automatically.

VII.2.2. CREATING AN EXCEL FILTER FOR A TEXT ELEMENT

Next, we want to filter and display companies that sell tires, regardless of where they are located in the world. To do this, we will enter the following formula:

=FILTER(A4:D18;C4:C18="Tires"). In again, here how understand it:

- *A4:D18* corresponds to the range taken into account in the operation, in this case the entire table,
- *C4:C18* corresponds to the range subject to our filtering criterion,
- *="Tires"* corresponds to our criterion.

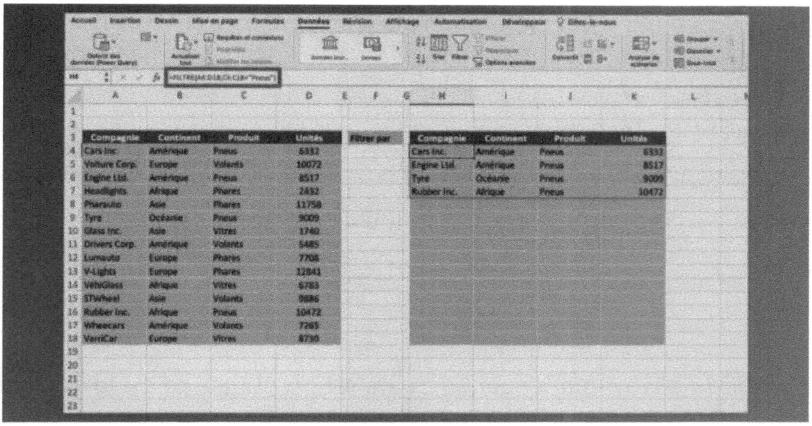

You can manually enter the element that determines the filter, enclosed in quotation marks.

There is another way to apply this filter. Instead of manually entering *"Tires"* in your formula, you can select a cell that contains your criterion. Below, , we have created a drop-down list so that we have our conditions at our fingertips. We then enter the formula *=FILTER(A4:D18;C4:C18=F4),* with cell F4 replacing the word "tires" since it is already entered there.

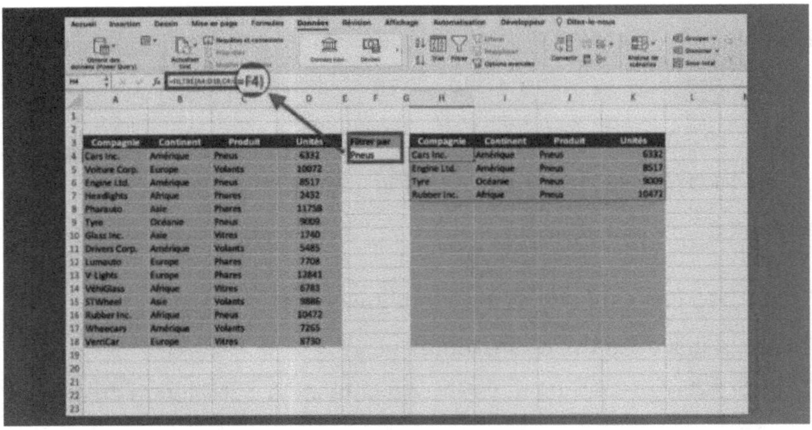

Here, cell F4 corresponds to the word "Tires."

VII.2.3. CREATING AN EXCEL FILTER BASED ON MULTIPLE CRITERIA

We now want to apply two conditions to our filter. In our example, we want to filter companies that sell 8,000 or more tires. So, still in cell H4 destination results, enter formula following :

Here its meaning:

- *A4:D18* always corresponds to the range of data to be taken into account,
- *(D4:D18>=8000)*(C4:C18="Tires")* corresponds to the two conditions already used in our previous examples. To correlate them , make sure to include both of them in parentheses and separate them with *the* * sign (asterisk or multiplier sign).

The filter is applied and shows you the companies that have sold more than 8,000 tires.

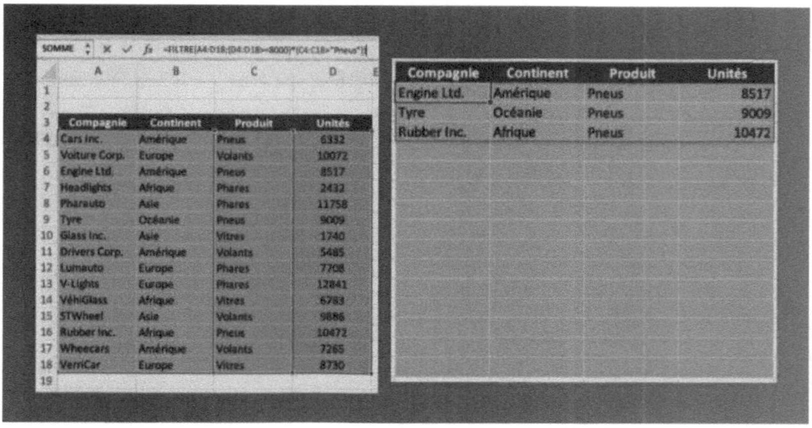

Compagnie	Continent	Produit	Unités
Cars inc.	Amérique	Pneus	6332
Voiture Corp.	Europe	Volants	10072
Engine Ltd.	Amérique	Pneus	8517
Headlights	Afrique	Phares	2432
Pharauto	Asie	Phares	11758
Tyre	Océanie	Pneus	9009
Glass Inc.	Asie	Vitres	1740
Drivers Corp.	Amérique	Volants	5485
Lumauto	Europe	Phares	7708
V-Lights	Europe	Phares	12841
VéhiGlass	Afrique	Vitres	6783
STWheel	Asie	Volants	9886
Rubber Inc.	Afrique	Pneus	10472
Wheecars	Amérique	Volants	7265
VerriCar	Europe	Vitres	8730

Compagnie	Continent	Produit	Unités
Engine Ltd.	Amérique	Pneus	8517
Tyre	Océanie	Pneus	9009
Rubber Inc.	Afrique	Pneus	10472

Two criteria are taken into account here, but you can apply more depending on your needs.

VII.2.4. CREATE AN EXCEL FILTER BASED ON AT LEAST ONE CRITERION

It is also possible to filter a table of data based on at least one criterion out of several requested. For example, after filtering, we want all European companies and all those that sell fewer than 9,000 units of products. The filter formula must be written so that we get all European companies regardless of their sales volume, as well as all companies from the rest of the world that sell less than 9,000 units. Here it is:

The only difference here is the use of the "+ " sign to tell your Excel filter that these two criteria are added independently and are not conditional on each other.

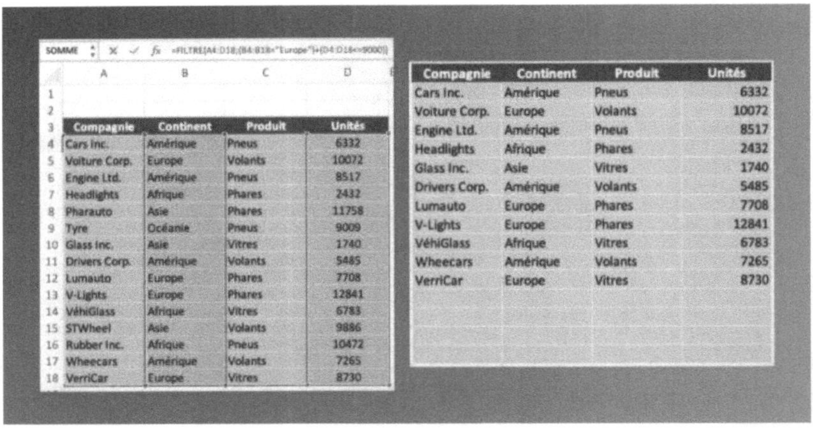

	Compagnie	Continent	Produit	Unités
4	Cars Inc.	Amérique	Pneus	6332
5	Voiture Corp.	Europe	Volants	10072
6	Engine Ltd.	Amérique	Pneus	8517
7	Headlights	Afrique	Phares	2432
8	Pharauto	Asie	Phares	11758
9	Tyre	Océanie	Pneus	9009
10	Glass Inc.	Asie	Vitres	1740
11	Drivers Corp.	Amérique	Volants	5485
12	Lumauto	Europe	Phares	7708
13	V-Lights	Europe	Phares	12841
14	VéhiGlass	Afrique	Vitres	6783
15	STWheel	Asie	Volants	9886
16	Rubber Inc.	Afrique	Pneus	10472
17	Wheecars	Amérique	Volants	7265
18	VerriCar	Europe	Vitres	8730

Compagnie	Continent	Produit	Unités
Cars Inc.	Amérique	Pneus	6332
Voiture Corp.	Europe	Volants	10072
Engine Ltd.	Amérique	Pneus	8517
Headlights	Afrique	Phares	2432
Glass Inc.	Asie	Vitres	1740
Drivers Corp.	Amérique	Volants	5485
Lumauto	Europe	Phares	7708
V-Lights	Europe	Phares	12841
VéhiGlass	Afrique	Vitres	6783
Wheecars	Amérique	Volants	7265
VerriCar	Europe	Vitres	8730

Here, we have European companies and those that sell at least 9,000 units.

VII.2.5 CREATING AN ADVANCED EXCEL FILTER WITH TWO CRITERIA

For this last example on Excel filters, we want to quickly obtain a list of companies that sell between 8,000 and 10,000 units of products. Thanks to the situations described above, we have all the knowledge we need to set up such a filter. Here is an of the formulas quot;quot;quot;quot;quot;quot;quot;quot;quot;quot;quot;quot;quot;quot;quot;quot;quot;quot;quot;quot;quot;quot;quot;quot;quot;quot;quot;quot;quot;quot;quot;quot;quot;quot;quot;quot;quot;quot;quot;quot;quot;quot;quot;quot;quot

: *=FILTER(A4:D18;(D4:D18>=8000)*(D4:D18<=10000))*. Its explanation

is:

- *A4:D18* corresponds to the entire data table,
- *(D4:D18>=8000)*(D4:D18<=10000)* corresponds to the combination of our two criteria, first the values located in column *D4:D18*

that are strictly greater than or equal to 8,000, and second the values that are strictly less than or equal to 10,000.

Once again, it is possible to dispense with the complete formulation that includes the signs>= by entering the data with filter criteria values in cells. Here, our minimum and maximum values have been entered in cells F6 and F8, which we can therefore use in the formula in this way :

=FILTER(A4:D18;(D4:D18>=F6)(D4:D18<=F8))*. Cells *F6* and *F8* thus replace the values *>=8000* and *<=10000.*

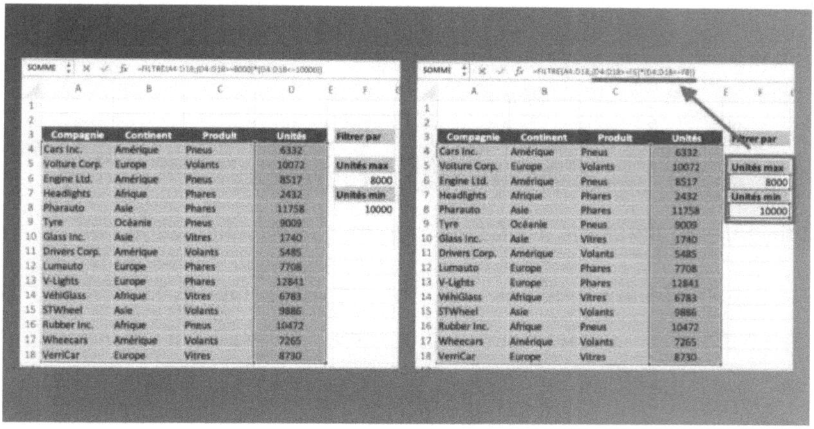

Here are two ways to write your formula.

VII.2.6. A FINAL TIP IF FILTERING DOES NOT WORK

You may set up a filter that does not return any results. To prevent Excel from displaying an error or to specify that no data was found that matches your filter, you can add a message to your formula yourself, using the " " command. To do this, simply add your short text in quotation marks at the end of the formula.

For example, we want our filter to give us the companies that sell 13,000 or more units of products. There are none, but let's assume that we don't know. We will therefore enter the appropriate formula for our filter, with a text for missing results: *=FILTER(A4:D18;D4:D18>=13000;"no results").*

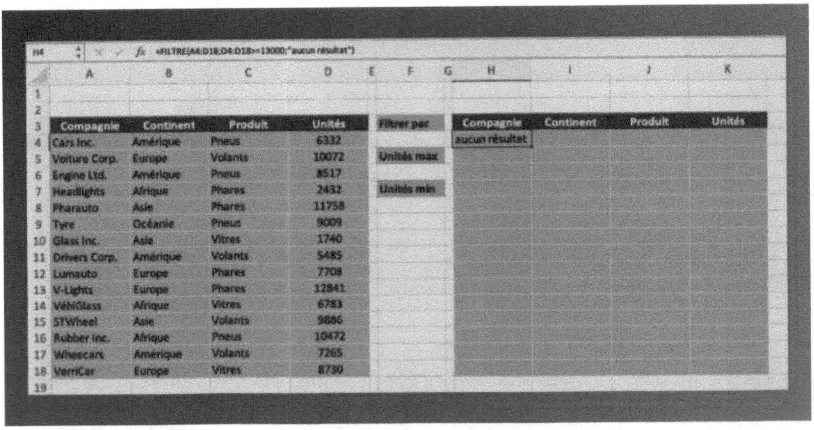

The pre-entered message is displayed in the filter's destination cell.

You can also specify that the field will remain empty if no results are found. To do this, the formula is the same, but instead of entering " ", enter " " between " " and ". " " Example :

CHAPTER VIII: DATA COLLECTION AND PROCESSING WITH MS EXCEL

To better represent the simplicity, speed, and more intuitive operation of Idées' data analysis, the feature has been **renamed Analyze Data**. The functionality and experience are identical and continue to align with the same privacy and license management regulations. If you are on the semi-annual Enterprise Channel, you may still see "Ideas" displayed as Excel until it is updated.

Analyze Data in Excel gives you a deep understanding of your data through natural language queries that let you ask questions about **your data without** having to write complex formulas. In addition, Analyze Data provides high-level visual summaries, trends, and patterns.

Simply select a cell in a data range > and choose the **Analyze Data** button in the **Home** tab. Analyze Data in Excel analyzes your data and returns interesting visuals about it in an Office pane.

If you are looking for more specific information, you can enter a question in the query box at the top of the pane, then press **Enter**. Data Analysis will provide answers with visuals such as tables, charts, or pivot tables that can then be inserted into the workbook.

If you're interested in exploring your data or just want to see what's possible, Data Analytics also provides personalized suggested questions that you can access by selecting them in the query box.

Try suggested questions Simply ask a question

Select the text box at the top of the Data Analysis pane to see a list of suggestions based on your data.

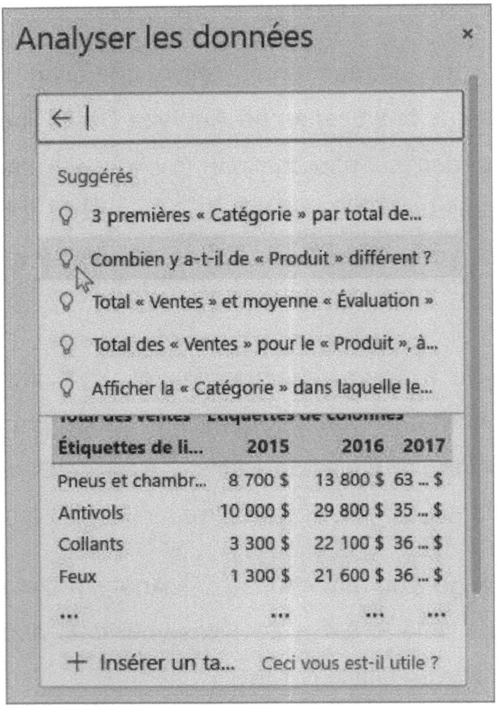

You can also enter a specific question about your data.

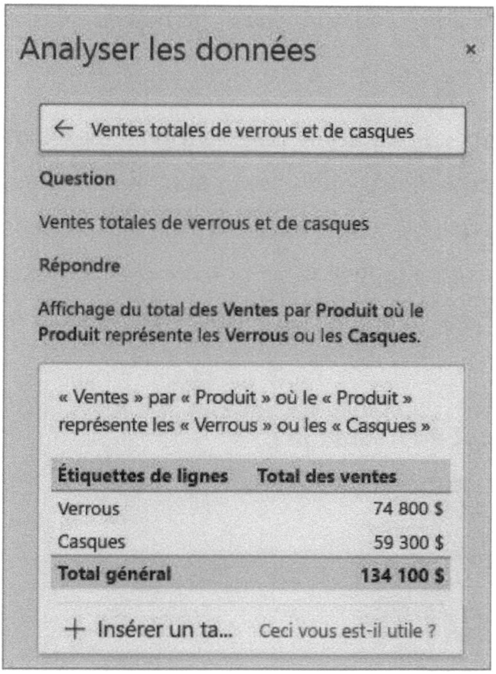

Note

- Analyze Data is available to Microsoftsubscribers 365 in English, French, Spanish, German, Simplified Chinese, and Japanese. If you are a Microsoft 365 subscriber, make sure you have the latest version of Office. To learn more about the different update channels for Office, see Overview of update channels for appsMicrosoft 365 .
- The natural language queries feature in Data Analytics is being rolled out to customers over time. It may not be available in all countries or regions at this time.

Getting specific information with Analyze Data

If you don't have a specific question in mind, in addition to natural language, Analyze Data analyzes and provides high-level visual summaries, patterns, and trends.

You can save time and get deeper analysis by selecting only the fields you want to see. When you choose fields and how to summarize them, Analyze Data excludes other available data, speeding up the process and presenting fewer, more focused suggestions. For example, you may only want to see total sales by year. You can also ask Analyze Data to show average sales by year.

Select **Which fields are you most interested in?**

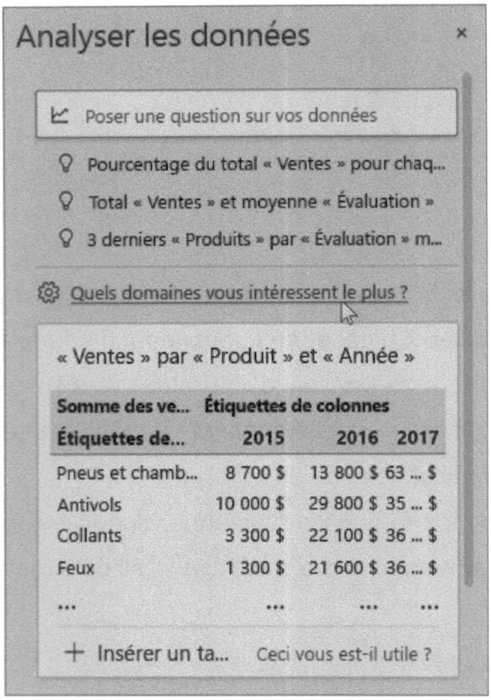

Select the fields and how you want to summarize their data.

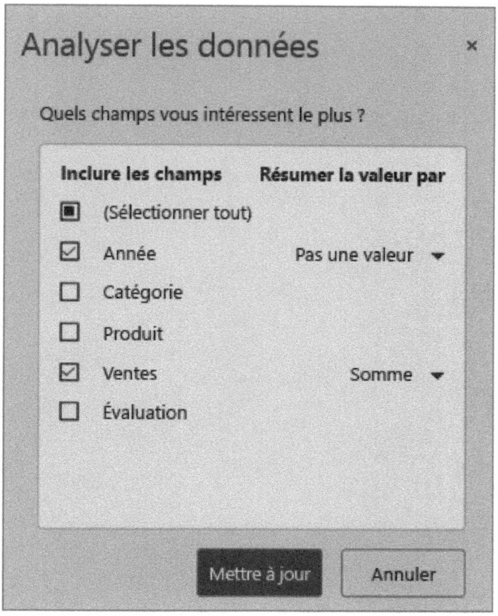

Analyze Data offers a smaller number of more targeted suggestions.

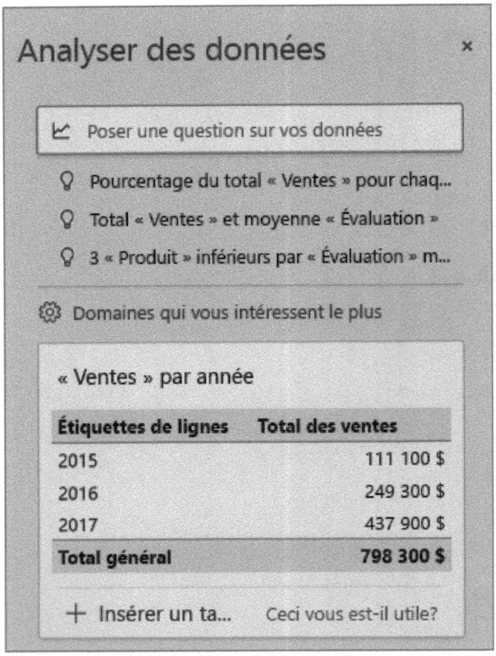

Note: The **Not a value** option in the field list refers to fields that are not usually added or calculated. For example, you do not calculate the year displayed, but you may want to add the values of the years shown. If you use it with another field that is summed or averaged, the **Not a value** option works as a row label. If used alone, **Not a value** counts the unique values in the selected field.

Analyzing data is more effective with clean, tabular data.

Année	Catégorie	Produit	Ventes	Évaluation
2017	Composants	Chaînes	200€	75 %
2015	Vêtements	Chaussettes	37€	22 %
2017	Vêtements	Cuissards	40€	22 %
2015	Vêtements	Shorts	133€	56 %
2017	Vêtements	Collants	360€	100 %
2015	Composants	Guidons	23€	35 %
2016	Vêtements	Chaussettes	23€	28 %
2016	Pièces détachée	Freins	34€	36 %
2016	Vélos	Vélos tout-terrai	63€	40 %
2017	Composants	Freins	54€	38 %
2016	Accessories	Casques	170€	90 %
2016	Accessories	Feux	216€	90 %
2016	Accessories	Antivols	298€	90 %
2016	Composants	Axes de pédalier	10€	23 %
2015	Vêtements	Maillots	67€	5 %
2017	Pièces détachée	Axes de pédalier	6€	27 %
2015	Vélos	Vélos de route	35€	50 %
2017	Vêtements	Maillots	75€	40 %
2017	Accessoires	Pneus et chambr	637€	90 %

Here are some tips for getting the most out of Analyze Data:

1. Analyze Data works best with data formatted as an Excel table. To create an Excel table, click anywhere in your data, then **press Ctrl+T**.
2. Make sure the column headers are correct. They should be a single row of unique, filled labels for each column. Avoid using double rows of headers, merged cells, etc.
3. If you are using complex or nested data, you can use Power Query to convert your tables into pivot tables or multiple rows of headers.

If you are unable to Analyze Data, the reason is probably on my end (Author Junior NKIERE) rather than yours.

Here are some reasons why Analyze Data may not work on your data:

- Analyze Data does not currently support analyzing datasets larger than 1.5 million cells. There is currently no workaround. In the meantime, you can filter your data, then copy it to another location to run Analyze Data on it.
- Strings such as "2017-01-01" will be analyzed as text strings. To resolve this issue, create a column that uses the DATE or DATEVAL functions and format its contents as a date.
- Analyzing data does not work when Excel is in compatibility mode (i.e., when the file is in .xls format). In the meantime, save your file as an .xlsx file,
.xlsm, or .xlsb file.
- Similarly, Ideas may have difficulty interpreting merged cells. If you are trying to centralize your data, such as in a report header, you can resolve this issue by deleting all merged cells and then formatting the cells with the Center in multiple columns option. Press **Ctrl+1**, then go to **Alignment> Horizontal> Center in multiple columns**.

CHAPTER IX: BASIC CONCEPTS OF ALGORITHMS AND CODING

Algorithms are the study and production of rules and techniques involved in defining and designing algorithms, i.e., systematic processes for solving problems that allow you to precisely describe the steps for solving an algorithmic problem.

An algorithm must be readable and understandable by several people. It

must therefore follow rules.

It consists of a **header** and a **body**:

- **the header,** which specifies: the name of the algorithm (Name:), its purpose (Role
:), the "input" data, i.e., the elements that are essential for its proper functioning (Input:), the "output" data, i.e., the elements calculated or produced by the algorithm (Output:), the local data essential to the algorithm (Declaration:)
- **the body**, which consists of: the start keyword, a series of indented instructions, the **end** keyword

EXAMPLE OF CODE

Name: addTwoIntegers
Role: Add two integers a and b and put the result in c Input: a,b: integer
Output: c: integer Declaration: - start
c ←a+b end

IX.1. VARIABLE

A variable is an entity that contains information:

- a variable has a name, called an identifier;

- a variable has a value;
- a variable has a type that characterizes the set of values that the variable can take;
- The set of variables are stored in the computer of the computer.

This can be likened to a filing cabinet containing labeled drawers:

- the cabinet would be the computer's memory;
- the drawers would be the variables (the label would correspond to the identifier);
- the contents of a drawer would be the value of the corresponding variable;
- the color of the drawer would be the type of variable (blue for invoices, red for purchase orders, etc.)

IX.2. VARIABLE TYPE

The type of a variable characterizes:

- the set of values that the variable can take;
- all the actions that can be performed on a variable

When a variable appears in the header of an algorithm, it is associated with a type using **the following syntax:**

Variable identifier: Its type For example:

age: Natural

name: Character string

- Once a data type is associated with a variable, that variable cannot change.
- Once a data type is associated with a variable, the content of that variable must be of the same type.

IX.3. DATA TYPE

For example, in the previous example, a and b were declared as integers

- a and b in this algorithm cannot store real numbers
- a and b in this algorithm cannot change type

There are two main categories of types:

- simple types
- complex types (which we will see later in the course).

A. SIMPLE TYPES

There are two main categories of simple types: Those with a finite number of elements, the countable types, and Those with an infinite number of elements, the uncountable types.

SIMPLE COUNTABLE TYPES

- **Boolean:** variables can only take the values TRUE or FALSE
- **Interval:** variables can only take integer values defined in this interval, for example 1..10
- **Enumerated**: variables can only take explicit values, for example the days of the week (Monday to Sunday).

These are the only simple types that can be defined by a computer science .

- **Characters**

EXAMPLES:

masculine: Boolean month: 1..12

day: DaysOfTheWeek

CASE OF ENUMERATIONS

If the programmer wants to use enumerated types, they must define the type in the algorithm header, specifying all the values of that type as follows:

type name= {value1, value2, ..., valueN} For example:

DaysOfTheWeek= {Monday, Tuesday, Wednesday, Thursday, Friday, Saturday, Sunday}

SIMPLE UNCOUNTABLE TYPES

- integer (positive and negative)
- natural (positive integers)
- real
- character string, for example 'course' or 'algorithmic' EXAMPLES:

age: natural size: real

name: character string

IX.4. OPERATOR, OPERAND, AND EXPRESSION

- **An operator** is an operation symbol that allows you to act on variables or perform "calculations."
- **An operand** is an entity (variable, constant, or expression) used by an operator.
- **An expression** is a combination of operator(s) and operand(s). It is evaluated during the execution of the algorithm and has a value (its interpretation) and a type.

For example, in a+b: a is the left operand

+ is the operator

b is the right operand

a+b is called an expression

If, for example, a is 2 and b is 3, the expression a+b is 5.

If, for example, a and b are integers, the expression a+b is an integer.

CHAPTER X: BASIC INSTRUCTIONS OF AN ALGORITHM

An **instruction** is a set of characters that defines, in a given programming language, a **basic operation** that a **computer** must perform. It is the most basic command that it can interpret.

To communicate with the machine, dialogue instructions (input/output instructions) must be used.

X.1. READ

Reading: there is an instruction that allows the user to enter values from the keyboard for use by the program.

The syntax of this read instruction is: (x is a variable)

In an algorithm: read x

When the program encounters an READ READ, the program stops running and waits for a value to be entered from the keyboard.

X.2. WRITE

- **Writing**: instruction that allows values to be communicated to the user by displaying them on the screen.

The syntax for this write instruction is:

```
                                        Ecrire  x
Dans un algorithme :
                            Ou     Ecrire  Expression
```

X.3. ASSIGNMENT

The assignment instruction is an operation that assigns a value to a variable. It is denoted by the symbol ← in algorithmic notation. This instruction is written as follows:

```
                                        VARIABLE ← valeur
Dans un algorithme :
                            Ou     VARIABLE ← EXPRESSION
```

Example 1:

AMOUNT← 3500

Write AMOUNT

Example 2:

B← 10

A← B

A← B * 2+ 5

Note: The order in which the instructions are written is essential to the final result.

Exercise: Write an algorithm that swaps the values of two variables A and B, regardless of their previous contents. The user is asked for the initial values, and the result of the swap is displayed.

Exercise: Write an algorithm that swaps the values of two variables A and B, regardless of their previous contents. Ask the user for the initial values and display the result of the swap.

X.4. BRANCHING

Branching instructions allow you to interrupt the normal flow of the program by jumping from one place in the program to another. This is why they are also called *jump instructions*.

BIBLIOGRAPHY

❖ **Works**

- Guide to support the Science Education Program, 8th grade basic education, 2019.
- Guillaume PLOUIN, *Cloud computing. Security, hybrid IS governance and market overview,* 4th edition, Dunod, Paris, 2016.
- Jacques LONCHAMP, Introduction to computer systems, Paris, Dunod, 2017.

❖ **Websites:**

- https://support.microsoft.com
- https://public.iutenligne.net
- https://www.emaze.com
- https://aws.amazon.com
- https://www.phpeasydata.com

TABLE OF CONTENTS